THE OFFICIAL BASEBALL HALL OF FAME

SCORE BOOK

Neil Cohen

LITTLE SIMON
Published by Simon & Schuster Inc.
New York

The views expressed in this book are solely
those of the author and do not necessarily
represent those of the Baseball Hall of Fame.

A BASEBALL INK BOOK

Note:

Quotations from Gary Carter (pp. 11–12 and 25), Mike Schmidt (pp. 14 and 23), Steve Garvey (p. 27), Ozzie Smith (pp. 13 and 37) and about Steve Carlton (p. 29) originally published in WOMAN'S DAY/PLAY BALL WITH LITTLE LEAGUE.

Quotations from Sandy Koufax (p. 36 and 53) and Joe Cronin (p. 51) reprinted with permission of Macmillan Publishing Company from BASEBALL FOR THE LOVE OF IT by Anthony J. Connor. Copyright © 1982 by Anthony J. Connor.

Quotations from Joe DiMaggio (pp. 14 and 41) from BASEBALL FOR EVERYONE by Joe DiMaggio. Copyright © 1948, by the McGraw-Hill Book Company.

Quotations from Carl Yastrzemski (p. 37), Bill Freehan (p. 43), and Tommy John (p. 41) from LITTLE LEAGUE TO BIG LEAGUE by Jim Brosnan. Copyright ©1968, by Random House, Inc. Reprinted by permission of the publisher.

Quotations from Pete Rose (pp. 9, 18, 33, and 47) from PETE ROSE'S WINNING BASEBALL by Pete Rose and Bob Hertzel. Copyright © 1976 by Pete Rose and Bob Hertzel. Reprinted by permission of Contemporary Books, Inc.

Quotations from Enos Slaughter (pp. 10 and 53), Roy Campanella (p. 23), and Phil Rizzuto (pp. 13 and 39) excerpted from HOW TO PLAY BIG LEAGUE BASEBALL, copyright 1951 by Malcolm Child, reprinted by permission of Harcourt Brace Jovanovich, Inc.

Quotation from Ty Cobb (p. 9) reprinted courtesy of Hillerich & Bradsby Co.

LITTLE SIMON
Simon & Schuster Building
Rockefeller Center
1230 Avenue of the Americas
New York, New York 10020
Copyright © 1989 by Professional Ink, Inc.
All rights reserved
including the right of reproduction
in whole or in part in any form.
LITTLE SIMON and colophon are trademarks
of Simon & Schuster Inc.
Manufactured in the United States of America
10 9 8 7 6 5 4 3 2 1
ISBN 0-671-67380-7

CONTENTS

A VISIT TO COOPERSTOWN

The National Baseball Hall of Fame and Museum is located in Cooperstown, New York. It is open all year round. But the biggest day is Hall of Fame Day in July or August, when the new members of the Hall are honored.

To be elected to the Hall of Fame is the greatest honor for a player, manager, umpire, or team or league official. A player must have played in the major leagues for ten seasons or more, and have been retired for at least five years to be eligible. Voting is done by the sportswriters who cover baseball and are members of the Baseball Writers Association of America. Players of many years past are reviewed for possible induction by the Veterans Committee.

The ceremony is always attended by many great retired players who are already in the Hall of Fame, as well as the baseball commissioner and league presidents. The next day, as part of the celebration, two major league teams play an exhibition game at nearby Doubleday Field.

Each Hall of Famer is honored with a bronze plaque in the Hall of Fame Gallery of the Museum. More than two hundred baseball greats are immortalized there.

The Hall of Fame is also a museum. It's like an art museum or a natural history museum, but it's all about baseball. Imagine that. Better yet, I'll help you imagine it. Let's take a tour.

On the first floor, we'll start with the Great Moments Room. This room lets us relive thrilling plays and events in baseball history with photographs that are bigger than life-size. There are original paintings of baseball scenes hanging on the walls, and televisions that play shows from *This Week in Baseball.*

Next stop is the Cooperstown Room, where we learn about the origin of the game and the history of the museum. The early days of baseball are shown in displays with photographs, original paintings, and an "interactive video" terminal that can answer many of your questions. Also in this room is what may be the oldest baseball in existence, the famous 150-year-old "Abner Doubleday baseball." At one time it was widely believed that Abner Doubleday invented baseball in Cooperstown in 1839. That is why the Hall of Fame was located here. Although today we are less certain about who invented baseball, Cooperstown remains the ideal symbolic spot for baseball's shrine.

Up the stairs, on the second floor, we find over 1,000 photographs and pieces of memorabilia showing the history of bat and ball games. Baseball got its start from an English game called rounders. But over the years, Americans began playing the game differently. In 1845, Alexander Cartwright and the Knickerbocker Base Ball Club created their first printed rules of baseball. Here you can trace baseball's history from those early days to today's teams and players.

Nearby is an exhibit all about baseball's annual All-Star Game, with game programs, newspaper clippings, tickets, and press pins.

Also on the second floor is a collection of artifacts and photographs in tribute to Casey Stengel, the player and manager who was the game's beloved goodwill ambassador for over fifty years. There is an impressive exhibit on the old Negro Leagues, before integration came to major-league baseball in 1947. And there is a Hank Aaron exhibit that shows his progress toward breaking Babe Ruth's home run record.

Let's go up to the third floor for a big favorite among dads, the Ballparks Room. Here we find original turnstiles, lockers, dugout benches, and grandstand seats from the great old ballparks of the past: Ebbets Field, the Polo Grounds, Forbes Field, Shibe Park, and Crosley Field.

There are displays of great moments in Playoff and Championship Series play, plus a World Series Room that brings back memories of great Fall Classics.

A collection of uniforms traces the evolution of the game's apparel from heavy, woolen flannels to today's colorful and light double knits.

And then there's Babe Ruth. The Hall boasts the world's largest collection of memorabilia and photographs of the game's greatest player. They even have his Yankee Stadium locker.

And for you baseball-card collectors, there is a unique collection of historic cards, including the rare Honus Wagner T-206 tobacco card.

Over in the new wing of the building is a display showing the evolution of equipment through the years. You will see that the bats, balls, gloves, and catchers' gear used by the game's pioneers look like they're from the Stone Age next to the equipment used by players today.

What about today's stars? you ask as we head downstairs. Well, tomorrow's Hall of Famers are also well represented by colorful photos in the lobby. And complete uniforms of today's major league teams can be found in the Baseball Today area in the new wing, which also houses a movie theater.

That's the National Baseball Hall of Fame and Museum. It's even better in person.

HOW TO KEEP SCORE

Do you remember your first big league baseball game? I remember mine. It was May 1963, at the old Polo Grounds in New York. The Mets were playing the Milwaukee Braves. I was 10 years old.

The scorecard I kept that day is old and torn now. Many of the pencil marks are smudged. But reading it, I see that the Braves had two future Hall of Famers on the field that day. Hank Aaron was in right field, and Eddie Mathews at third base. The Mets, however, had the hero that day. First baseman Tim Harkness won the game for New York in the sixteenth inning with a home run.

That is one of the great things about keeping score. You can look back at your scorecard days, weeks, even years later, and know exactly what happened in a game.

If you keep score for your own league team, a scorecard can tell you how many hits each player on the team had that day and how many runs each pitcher gave up. Then you can figure out statistics, such as batting average and earned run average.

At a big league game, keeping score will help you understand what is happening on the field. You will be an expert, just like the announcers on TV. They are keeping score too.

Keeping score is easy. The important thing to remember is that you will want to write things down in a way so that you'll be able to read them back later on. To do that, baseball scorers use a system of symbols, letters, and numbers that were invented by Henry Chadwick, the first man to write regularly about baseball in the newspapers, way back in the 1850s.

First I'll tell you what the symbols are, then I'll show you how to use them.

Who's on First

We can't fit their names into those little boxes, so, once the game begins, we refer to the players by numbers. These are not their uniform numbers but the numbers of the positions they play in the field:

1—Pitcher
2—Catcher
3—First Baseman
4—Second Baseman
5—Third Baseman
6—Shortstop
7—Left Fielder
8—Center Fielder
9—Right Fielder

So far, so good. The only place it gets tricky is with the shortstop. The reason why the shortstop is 6 instead of 5 has been lost with history. But the best explanation is that in the early days of baseball the shortstop was considered more of a shallow outfielder than an infielder.

The numbers are used to show which fielders handled the ball after the batter hit it. For example, if the batter hits a ground ball to the shortstop, who throws to the first baseman to make the out, we score that 6-3. If the batter hits a fly ball to the center fielder, who catches it for an out, we write down the number 8.

Breaking the Code

Letters and symbols are used to show what happened to a hitter during his time at bat. Here are all the symbols you need to score a ballgame:

1B—single
2B—double
3B—triple
HR—home run
K—strikeout, swinging
Я—strikeout, called
BB—walk
BB—intentional walk
HBP—hit by pitch
WP—wild pitch
PB—passed ball
SB—stolen base
CS—caught stealing
BK—balk
E—error
F—foul out
SAC—sacrifice bunt
SF—sacrifice fly
P—pop fly
G—ground out, unassisted
L—line drive out
DP—double play

The symbols are easy to remember because they look and sound just like the plays they describe. Most of the letters we use are just the first letter of the word for that play. We mark *K* for a strikeout because *S* is already used in sacrifice and sacrifice fly. Besides, *K* "sounds" more like a strikeout.

Sometimes scorekeepers use letters with numbers to give more detail about a play. If a batter hit a ground ball to the first baseman, who picks it up and steps on first base, we would score it 3G. A pop fly out to the first baseman would be 3P. If a batter hits a hard line drive at the third baseman, then it's 5L. A double play from the shortstop to the second baseman to the first baseman would be DP 6-4-3.

Bases in the Box

In some ways, keeping score is just like playing baseball.

You can see on the sample scorecard on the following page that there is a row of squares next to where we write each player's name. Each square is for an inning.

Imagine each square is a miniature baseball diamond, with first base in the lower right corner, second base in the upper right corner, third base in the top left, and home plate in the bottom left.

When we write in the box what that batter does in an inning, we trace his progress around the square in just the way he moves around the bases. How he reached base is marked in the first-base corner, how he reached second in the second-base corner, how he reached third in the third, and who drove him in or how he scored in the last one. When a batter reaches first, I always divide the box into quarters. That makes it easier to follow the action.

Putting It All Together

To show you how the numbers, letters, and boxes work together, I've scored three innings of an imaginary game. I'll give the play-by-play in words here, and show you how I marked the same play-by-play in scoring shorthand on my scorecard.

The team that we'll be watching is the 1961 New York Yankees, one of the greatest ballclubs of all time. The Bronx Bombers won 109 games that year, to win the American League pennant, then whipped the Cincinnati Reds 4–1 in the World Series. Roger Maris hit a record-breaking 61 home runs, and Mickey Mantle was close behind, with 54. Three Hall of Famers (Mantle, Yogi Berra, and Whitey Ford) are in the starting nine.

The first thing we do before the game begins is to fill in the starting lineup and the position each batter will play today. Bobby Richardson leads off, playing second base, followed by shortstop Tony Kubek. Maris (right field), Mantle (center field), and Elston Howard (catcher) bat in the three, four, and five positions. Then come first baseman Bill "Moose" Skowron, catcher Yogi

Berra, and third baseman Clete Boyer. Batting ninth, in these days before the designated hitter, is pitcher Whitey Ford.

Remember, we will be referring to each player in the scorecard according to the number of his position.

Now, let's play ball.

First inning. Richardson leads off with a single to left field, so we mark in the first-base (bottom right) corner of his box 1B for his hit and the small number 7, to show us that the hit went to left field. We also divide up the box in case he moves around the bases.

Sure enough, while Kubek is at bat, Richardson steals second base. We record this by writing SB in his second-base corner, along with the small number 6, which tells us that he stole while the shortstop, Kubek, was batting. Kubek grounds to the second baseman, who throws him out at first, moving Richardson to third. We mark 4-3 in Kubek's box (no need to divide it here), and write the number 6 in the third-base corner of Richardson's box to show that he advanced to third on Kubek's play.

Next up is Roger Maris, who hits a long fly ball to right field that allows Richardson to tag up at third and score. Maris gets a 9SF in his box, for sacrifice fly to the right fielder. We also write Maris's number 9 in the home-plate corner of Richardson's box, to show that Richardson scored a run and was driven in by Maris.

Mickey Mantle strikes out swinging, to end the inning (K). Notice that I've drawn a little slash under Mantle's first-inning scoring box. That will remind me where in the lineup to start scoring when the Yankees come to bat in the second inning.

At the bottom of each inning, there is another box marked R/H, to help us keep track of how many runs scored on how many hits in the inning. We mark 1 in the R part of the box, and 1 in the H part.

Second inning. Catcher Elston Howard leads off, and hits a double to right field (2B-9). First baseman Moose Skowron hits a ball to the first baseman, which he boots

PLAYER	POS	1	2	3
Richardson	④ 2B	6|5B⁸ 9|1B⁷	1L	
Kubek	⑥ SS	4-3		9|BK⁹ 9|BB
Maris	⑨ RF	9SF		HR⁹
Mantle	⑧ CF	K		3B⁷
Howard	② C		3|2B⁹ 7|♪	|BB
Skowron	③ 1B		1|7 E-3	⅄₁
Berra	⑦ LF		1|1B⁸	DP 6-4-3
Boyer	⑤ 3B		6P	
Ford	⓪ P		SAC 1-3	
	R/H	1/1	1/2	2/2

for an error (E-3), allowing Howard to move to third (note the 3 for Skowron in the third-base corner of Howard's box).

Yogi Berra singles to center (1B-8), scoring Howard (we mark Berra's 7 in Howard's home-plate corner) and moving Skowron to second (also marked 7).

Third baseman Clete Boyer pops up to the shortstop (6P). Pitcher Whitey Ford, who will win 25 games this year, lays down a sacrifice bunt (SAC 1-3), moving Berra to second and Skowron to third (note the number 1 in those corners of their boxes).

Richardson comes up again and lines one right back to the pitcher, who snags it (1L). And we close the Yankees' half of the second by noting at the bottom that they scored 1R on 2H.

Third inning. Kubek leads off with a walk (BB). While Maris is at bat, the pitcher commits a balk (BK-9) and Kubek is awarded second base. Maris then hits a home run to right field (HR-9), scoring Kubek ahead of him (mark 9 in Kubek's third-base and home-plate corners). Up comes Mickey Mantle, who hits a triple to left field (3B-7).

Here, the opposing team brings in a relief pitcher. We note that with a heavy black line

under Mantle's box to remind us that the following batters belong to the new pitcher. Howard walks (BB), and Skowron strikes out looking (Я). It is the new pitcher's first strikeout, so we mark a small number 1 next to the K. Berra grounds into a double play, from the shortstop to the second baseman to the first baseman (DP 6-4-3).

The Yankees are out in the third, but not before they scored 2 runs on 2 hits.

Last Licks

Although they are not shown here, on the far right side of each scorecard in this book you will find another 5 columns. These are marked AB (at-bats), R (runs scored), H (hits made), BB (walks), and TB (total bases). This is where you can record the game totals for each batter.

There is also a place for pitchers' game totals at the bottom right of the scorecard. There you will find columns for IP (innings pitched), H (hits allowed), R (runs allowed), ER (earned runs allowed), BB (walks), and SO (strikeouts). When you are determining which runs were earned, remember that runs that score as a result of a fielding error are unearned.

You can keep track of season totals in all of these categories on the special stat sheets on pages 54 and 55.

* * *

Got all that? Keeping score is not so hard. And it's really up to you how much or how little detail you want to put into your scoring. You can make up some of your own symbols. You can even write notes in the margins.

Just remember, you keep score to help you remember what happened in a game. So it doesn't have to be perfect, and it doesn't have to be neat, just as long as you will be able to read what you wrote later on. And if you forget any of the symbols, or how to write them in the box, don't panic, don't worry. Just turn to these pages and we'll go through it all again.

Baseball statistics are a lot more fun than they sound. Let's call them stats instead. That's better.

There are some stats that you just count up. For batters, those are hits, walks, runs batted in, runs scored, and home runs. For pitchers, they are wins, losses, strikeouts, earned runs, and walks.

Other stats are a little more complicated. But they're not hard when you know the formulas.

Batting Average

Batting average (BA) measures how often a batter gets a basehit. To determine a hitter's BA, divide the total number of hits by the total times at bat (walks, sacrifices, and being hit by a pitch do not count as times at bat; reaching base on an error does).

HITS/AT-BATS = BATTING AVERAGE

Example: In his first 95 at-bats during the 1949 season, defending American League batting champion and future Hall of Famer Ted Williams had 35 hits (this is not really so; we're just using the number as an example). What was Williams's batting average so far that season?

35 (Hits)/95 (At-Bats) =
.368 Batting Average

The last major leaguer to hit .400 in a season was Williams, who hit .406 back in 1941. Since then, George Brett has come the closest, with .390 in 1980. Any player who can hit .300 is considered an excellent hitter. That shows that hitting is a hard thing to do. Even the best fail 7 out of 10 times.

On-Base Average

On-base average (OBA) is batting average with walks, being hit by a pitch, and sacri-fice flies added in. OBA measures a player's ability to become a baserunner.

OBA is not as hard to figure out as it looks. It has a three-step formula:

1. HITS + WALKS + HIT BY PITCH =
   TOTAL TIMES ON BASE
2. AT-BATS + WALKS + HIT BY PITCH
   + SACRIFICE FLIES =
   TOTAL PLATE APPEARANCES
3. TOTAL TIMES ON BASE/TOTAL PLATE
   APPEARANCES = ON-BASE AVERAGE

Example: Ty Cobb, who played from 1905 to 1928, would do anything to help his team win. Let's say that in the 1915 season, through his first 115 at-bats, Cobb had 41 hits, had walked 15 times, had been hit by a pitched ball twice, and had 5 sacrifice flies. What would his OBA be?

1. 41 (Hits) + 15 (Walks) + 2 (Hit by Pitch)
   = 58 Times on Base
2. 115 (At-Bats) + 15 (Walks) + 2 (Hit by
   Pitch) + 5 (Sacrifice Flies) =
   137 Total Plate Appearances
3. 58 (Times on Base)/137 (Total Plate Appearances) = .423 On-Base Average

Your OBA will tend to be higher than your batting average. How much higher will depend on how good an eye you have at the plate. In 1987, Tim Raines of the Montreal Expos had a batting average of .330 and walked 90 times. His on-base average was an excellent .429. So you see, in the world of OBA, a walk is indeed as good as a hit.

Slugging Average

Slugging average (SLG) measures a batter's ability to get extra-base hits. SLG is the total bases a batter has hit for divided by his total at-bats. A batter gets one base for every single he hits, two bases for every double, three bases for every triple, and four bases for every home run.

TOTAL BASES/TOTAL AT-BATS = SLUGGING AVERAGE

Example: Let's take a look at the first month of an imaginary season for Hall of Famer Hank Aaron, one of the greatest sluggers of all time, with 755 career home runs. After 88 at-bats, Aaron had hit 15 singles, 4 doubles, 2 triples, and 7 home runs. How do we figure out Aaron's slugging average?

First, we add up his total bases:

15 singles × 1 base   = 15
4 doubles × 2 bases   = 8
2 triples × 3 bases   = 6
7 home runs × 4 bases = 28
Total bases   = 57

Then we plug our numbers into the formula:

57 (TB)/88 (AB) =
.648 SLG

The more extra-base hits a batter has, the higher his slugging average will be. Don Mattingly of the Yankees had a slugging percentage of .559 in 1987. Mattingly had 116 singles, but he also had 38 doubles, 2 triples, and 30 home runs.

Production

As you see, there are many ways to measure how well a player hits. Which is the best? That's hard to say, because each one—BA, SLG, and OBA—measures a different part of the game. But you can combine slugging average and on-base average and come up with a stat called production. A player who has a high production score will be one who excels in all aspects of batting: hitting for power, hitting for average, and getting a lot of walks. That sounds like a Most Valuable Player.

SLUGGING AVERAGE + ON-BASE AVERAGE = PRODUCTION

Example: Let's see how well this formula works. In 1987, Wade Boggs of the Red Sox

posted a .588 slugging average and a .461 on-base average. His production?

.588 (SLG) + .461 (OBA) =
1.049 Production

Meanwhile, George Bell, the American League's leading home run hitter, racked up a .605 slugging average and a .352 on-base average. His production was .957. Boggs was not the slugger that Bell was, but his production was greater because he had a much higher OBA. And though Bell was voted the American League's Most Valuable Player, this stat shows that Boggs was the more productive hitter.

Game-Winning RBI

The game-winning RBI is the RBI in a game that gives a team a lead that it never loses. It could be a sacrifice fly in the first inning of a 10–0 rout, or a home run in the bottom of the last inning that breaks a tie.

You don't need a formula for this one. Just keep track of who gets the game-winning RBI (GWRBI) on your scorecard.

Earned Run Average

Earned run average (ERA) is the average number of earned runs a pitcher would give up if he pitched a complete game. It separates his performance from how well his teammates hit or fielded behind him.

To figure ERA, we count up the total number of runs earned off a pitcher's pitching and divide it by the total number of innings he has pitched. Then we multiply that number by the number of innings in an official league game (nine).

1. TOTAL EARNED RUNS/TOTAL INNINGS PITCHED = EARNED RUNS PER INNING

2. EARNED RUNS PER INNING × INNINGS IN COMPLETE GAME = EARNED RUN AVERAGE

Example: Let's say that Hall of Famer Sandy Koufax got off to a strong start in the 1964 season and allowed just 5 earned runs in his first 21 innings of pitching. To figure Koufax's earned run average, we have to follow two steps:

1. 5 (ER)/21 (Innings) =
    .238 (Runs per Inning)
2. .238 (RPI) × 9 (Innings in a Complete Big League Game) =
    2.14 Earned Run Average

Another example. This time you'll be the pitcher. You've pitched 12 innings this season and given up five runs. A complete game in your league may be 6 or 7 innings long, but we'll stick with the 9-inning standard. What is your earned run average?

1. 6 (ER)/12 (Innings) =
    .50 (Runs per Inning)
2. .50 (RPI) × 9 (Innings in a Game) =
    4.50 ERA

In the big leagues, an ERA under 4.00 is good. An ERA under 3.00 is excellent. A pitcher who can keep his ERA under 2.00 is bound for Cooperstown.

In 1968, Hall of Famer Bob Gibson of the St. Louis Cardinals had one of the lowest earned run averages in baseball history. It was 1.12.

In 1987, future Hall of Famer Nolan Ryan had an ERA of 2.76, the lowest in the National League that season. But Ryan's record was only 8–16. That tells us that Ryan didn't get very much hitting or fielding support from his Houston Astros teammates. He pitched much better than his win-loss record shows. That's what ERA is all about.

Saves

A relief pitcher gets credit for a save if he comes into a close game that his team is winning and finishes the game without letting the other team tie the score. The rules say he must pitch with the player who represents the tying run on base, at bat, or on deck (or he must pitch the final three or more innings of a game his team wins).

There is no formula needed for figuring saves. You can keep track of them on your scorecard during the season.

Winning Percentage

The winning percentage for a pitcher tells us what percentage of his decisions he has won. To figure this out, first we add up his wins and losses to find his total decisions. Then we divide his wins by his decisions.

1. WINS + LOSSES =
    DECISIONS
2. WINS/DECISIONS =
    WINNING PERCENTAGE

Example: Let's say that at the start of the 1950 season, Hall of Fame pitcher Bob Lemon was 5–3 for his team, the Cleveland Indians. What would his winning percentage be?

1. 5 (Wins) + 3 (Losses) =
    8 (Decisions)
2. 5 (Wins)/8 (Decisions) =
    .625 Winning Percentage

One of the best winning percentages ever was posted by Ron Guidry of the Yankees in 1978. Guidry was 25–3 that year, for a percentage of .893. In 1987, Roger Clemens of the Red Sox was 20–9, for a percentage of .690. Clemens won more than two-thirds of his decisions, making him a valuable pitcher, indeed.

Team Winning Percentage

A team's winning percentage tells us what percent of its total games the team has won. To figure that out for your team, just divide wins by total games played.

WINS/TOTAL GAMES =
    TEAM WINNING PERCENTAGE

Example: Let's say the 1927 Yankees, one of the greatest teams in baseball history, won 10 games and lost 2 to start the season. What would their winning percentage be?

10 (Wins)/12 (Games) = .833.

When we say a team is at .500, we mean it has won half of its games. Anything over .500 is good. The 1986 Mets, with their record of 108–54, had a .667 team winning percentage. In 1987, the Minnesota Twins were 85–77. Their winning percentage was .525, the lowest for a World Champion in baseball history.

Even though the Twins had such a low winning percentage and the Mets had such a high one, they both were equally World Champions. That just goes to show you: Statistics tell a lot, but they don't tell everything.

HOW TO PLAY BASEBALL
Tips from today's stars and the all-time greats

How to Hit

Pete Rose on finding a batting stance:

"Be comfortable when you pick a stance. I take a deep crouch. My feet are a little farther apart than the average spread, about shoulder-width or a little farther.... Your hands must be kept back. About eight inches from the body is plenty.... Stand close enough to the plate so that you can cover the outside corner with the meat part of the bat."

Keeping your eye on the ball:

"From the moment that baseball leaves the pitcher's hand until you have to hit, there is nothing else in the world."

Swinging the bat:

"You begin with the stride.... I take a small stride, about six inches, and try to keep my weight on my back foot until the last possible moment....

"As you move forward, the hands remain back and cocked. This is the secret to hitting. The hands must remain uncommitted until the final second. As you begin striding, the hips begin opening, leading the way.

"I believe in a level swing, possibly even somewhat on a downward arc. The hands start from the top, about shoulder-high. I throw my hands right out front and then go on through. The idea is to hit the ball out front of the plate.

"As contact is made with the baseball, the arms are fully extended. The head remains on the ball. Your weight is transferred to the front foot. The wrists remain unbroken until after contact is made with the ball. They roll only after the ball has been hit, giving you the proper follow-through."

Ty Cobb on hitting to all fields:

"A righthanded batter attempting to hit to right, or the opposite, field should use the closed stance. That means the left foot is about four inches closer to the plate than the right. Hitting to left field, his front foot is about four inches farther away, or in open stance. The straightaway hitter lines up both feet with the line of the pitch."

Babe Ruth on taking batting practice:

"Every batter has some weakness, some kind of pitch that he cannot hit so well as other kinds. When a player is practicing batting, he should have his pitcher throw him the kind of ball that gives him the most trouble, so that he may overcome that weakness."

Breaking out of a slump:

"The best hitters in the game suffer from slumps. The only cure is to keep on swinging until the slump disappears."

Enos Slaughter on bunting:

"Assume your natural batting stance. When the ball has left the pitcher's hand, shift your feet so your body is almost facing the pitcher. Your arms and hands are loose, and you slide your forward hand along the bat until it is even with the trademark. You can hit to any side of the infield simply by turning your bat and the upper half of your body."

How to Run the Bases

Lou Brock on getting out of the batter's box:

"After you hit the ball, don't stand there and admire it. Get down to first in a hurry."

Running the bases:

"Practice rounding the bases. Try to touch the inside corner of the bag with your left foot."

Being alert:

"[When you're batting] know where the outfielders are playing. If they're deep on you, think about stretching that single into a double. . . . [When you're on base] be ready to take off on a wild pitch, passed ball, or error.

Ty Cobb on stealing:

"Watch the pitcher's feet and shoulders. If he uses his right arm in pitching, watch his left foot. You can tell by the position of his left foot whether he intends to throw to the plate or the base. If the pitcher is a lefthander, watch his right foot. Pitchers have other telltale movements.

"Study the catchers. Learn just how fast a catcher can throw, and what his weaknesses are.

"Keep the pitcher and the catcher guessing. If you always go on the first pitch, or

the second or third, they will soon be prepared to catch you in your attempt to steal."

Sliding:

"Some boys dive into the bag, sliding headfirst. Do not do this; slide feetfirst. When you slide feetfirst, you are less liable to be stepped on. . . . Go into a bag hard. Judge the distance. To slide properly you must learn to judge distance properly."

How to Pitch

Bob Lemon on the windup and delivery:

"I'm a righthander, so I toe the rubber with my right foot, placing my left foot a few inches behind the rubber. It's important that a pitcher develop a style so he can throw every pitch exactly the same way. I find I get a better rhythm [when I use] a windup, a sort of rocking motion with my two hands together in front of me.

"When I'm ready to pitch, I step toward the plate with my left foot. It's a long step, with knee bent. After releasing the ball, I swing my right leg around to a spot almost parallel with my left. In this way, I'm ready to field a ball hit back at me."

Pitching from the stretch position:

"The delivery with men on base is the same, but the starting position is different. You must have your right foot on the rubber, and your feet should be spread out as you face third base. The ball is hidden by the glove. With both hands together at eye level to start, you bring your right arm back to start the throw, stride toward the plate with your left. When you release the ball, get in position to field on the follow-through."

Carl Hubbell on throwing a fastball:

"Grip [the ball] tightly, with index and middle fingers on top and the thumb underneath. The fingers are usually placed across the seams, but, if along them, then at the place where the seams are closest together. When pitched, the ball rolls from under the fingers. This reverse rotation gives the ball backspin, causing it to 'hop.'"

Throwing a changeup:

"The change of pace differs from the fastball only in the manner in which it is held. Where the fastball is gripped tightly, the [changeup] is only lightly held by the fingers on top. Some pitchers lift these guiding fingers slightly as they let the ball go."

Tom Seaver on fielding your position:

"With no runners on base, simply stop the ball. Knock it down with an open glove, retrieve it, and make a sure throw to first base.

"In throwing to bases, accuracy is more important than speed. Make the throw chest-high, to give your infielder greater range in which to catch the ball and so that he can get out of the way of baserunners sliding in."

Covering first base:

"On any ball hit to the right side of the infield, it is the pitcher's responsibility to break to cover the first-base bag. Run to first base on a diagonal path from the mound until you are about eight to ten feet from the bag and parallel to the first-base foul line. Keep your glove raised to chest level to provide a good target."

Keeping baserunners close:

"Establish a point in your mind at which you will not let the runner advance in his lead. If he goes past that point, throw to first, driving him back to the bag.

"The best pickoff throw is a quick wrist flip aimed below your first baseman's knee and to the inside of the bag, so he can apply a quick tag."

How to Play Catcher

Bill Dickey on where to play:

"By playing as close as possible to the batter, the catcher is less likely to miss foul tips, gets into the best position to throw on steals, is best situated to catch low pitches in the strike zone, and is poised to break for a bunt."

Fielding pop fouls:

"Flip off your mask immediately and toss it in the opposite direction from the ball. Practice catching high fouls, because the ball has terrific spin as it hits the mitt."

Roy Campanella on calling pitches:

"Since you call for every pitch, you must know what type of pitch every man who comes to bat hits, and where he hits it. You should also find out each batter's weaknesses; what type of pitch he has the most trouble hitting."

Tagging a runner at the plate:

"The first thing you do is get rid of your mask and set yourself at the plate as a target for the outfielder's throw. When you have the ball, shift around to face the runner. Hold the ball in your bare hand and your glove so that it will not be knocked loose when the man comes sliding into you. Grab that ball first, then tag the runner."

Gary Carter on being ready to catch anything:

"A catcher must find himself a comfortable stance with good balance, and learn to shift his feet with the pitch. That's important for blocking balls in the dirt. Get both knees on the ground when a ball is in the dirt."

Throwing out baserunners at second:

"Have smooth action in coming into position for a throw to second base. Accuracy is

11

more important than the speed with which the ball gets there. Accuracy comes by practicing a lot."

How to Play First Base

Lou Gehrig on proper footwork around the bag:

"[Position yourself] with each heel touching an inside corner of the bag. They shouldn't be on the bag, as many boys wrongly think; they should be merely against it. From this position, it's easy to shift to get balls thrown to one side or the other. [If] a ball is thrown over to the left, you shift so that your right heel is against the left corner of the bag. That brings your body over to the left, and you can take the throw.

"[I use] this position because it gives me half the bag and the runner half; if I keep to my half and he to his, there's little danger that I'll be spiked."

Tagging the runner on a pickoff play:

"Learn to swing your arm down when you take a throw from the pitcher and tag a runner on his legs or feet. Then, whether he comes into the base upright or sliding, you're sure to touch him. The ball should be gripped tightly, for runners often try to knock a ball out of a baseman's hand."

George Sisler on stretching for the throw:

"On close plays, stretch forward as far as possible to catch the ball. The last portion of the foot to touch the bag is the toe, and not the heel, because if you try to stretch with only the heel on the bag, it certainly will come off. If the throw is bad, by all means leave the bag and make the catch."

Throwing to the pitcher covering first:

"When fielding a ball so that the pitcher has to cover first, throw the ball to him under-

handed and while moving toward him. Aim the toss chest-high and never conceal the ball from him."

Keith Hernandez on turning the 3-6-3 double play:

"The key is not to worry about the throw. It's remarkable how many first basemen throw the ball and then watch it. If I've thrown it bad, why watch it? So now I throw and beeline it back to the bag."

Scooping a throw out of the dirt:

"The real secret of scooping is using my bare hand and bringing it to the heel of my glove. Many times on halfway hops I actually catch the ball with my palm."

How to Play Second Base

Eddie Collins on where to play:

"As a general rule, the second baseman should play nearer second base than first base. More balls are hit near second. The hardest play a second baseman has to make is on balls hit over second base. It is easier to go to your left than to your right. And when you go to your left, you are always in a better position to make the throw to first."

Teaming up with the shortstop:

"Learn to work with your shortstop. Have a complete understanding with him on all plays. Decide between yourselves who is to cover second base on certain plays."

Rogers Hornsby on pivoting on the double play:

"When a double play is hoped for, you must move toward second base so as to be in position to cover that bag in time for the double play. To pivot correctly, always try to touch the bag with your right foot, then step with the left foot in toward the pitcher's mound and make the throw to first."

Taking the relay throw:

"When a ball is hit to right or right center for extra bases, the second baseman should run out to take the relay throw. Make up your mind, as you dash out, how many bases the ball will be good for, and you'll know where to relay the ball."

Pete Rose on starting the double play:

"The second baseman isn't always the middleman. Often he has to start the DP. Take the ball out of the glove, show it to the shortstop, and make the underhand flip if less than ten feet from the base, or a three-quarter throw if farther away."

Tagging a runner at second:

"It is the second baseman's job to cover second on a steal when a righthanded hitter is up. Get there as quickly as possible and straddle the bag. Catch the ball and snap it down on the inside of the base, letting the man slide into the ball."

Running down pop flies:

"On pop flies down the line behind first, the second baseman must take charge. He has a better angle than the first baseman."

How to Play Shortstop

Ozzie Smith on fielding hard-hit balls:

"I charge 'em. I'm not afraid of the ball. It won't bite you. I field the ball near the instep of my left foot, glove the ball, bring it up to my belt buckle, get my balance, and

throw to first, if that's where the play is. . . . You must get your body in front of the ball."

Honus Wagner on making the toughest play:

"The hardest play for a shortstop to make is going to his right for a deeply hit ball. Set yourself when you get your hands on the ball, and be in a position to throw to first."

Turning the double play:

"Remember, it is wiser to make sure of one out than to lose two. Grab the ball and feed it to the second baseman letter-high. If it's a grounder near second, flip it underhand to the second baseman.

"When pivoting in a double play, be in motion when receiving the ball, step on second base with the right foot, and remain on balance by stepping forward with the left before throwing to first."

Taking charge on pop flies:

"Size up a pop fly and yell for it as soon as you feel sure you can get it; otherwise, yell for either the left or center fielder to take it."

Phil Rizzuto on charging the slow roller:

"A slow roller is tougher to field than a hard grounder because you must run in faster and throw it while you are on the move. Although many infielders use only the bare hand, I field the ball with both my glove and bare hand. You do not lose too much time doing it this way, and it is much safer."

Taking the relay throw:

"On any ball hit safely into left field, your first duty is to run out for a possible relay from the outfielder back into the infield. On any ball hit to right field, you cover second while the second baseman goes out for the relay."

13

How to Play Third Base

Pie Traynor on where to play:

"In general, it is best to play behind the baseline. . . . Range as far as possible on grounders to your left. . . . Move up against a lefthanded batter or notorious bunter. When the batter snaps into the bunt posture, the third baseman should be charging in even before the pitch reaches the plate."

Making the throw:

"Many hard smashes reach the third baseman before the hitter has broken out of the batter's box. That leaves plenty of time for the throw. The baseman should straighten his body, take aim, cock his arm, and coordinate his throw with the stride. When the third baseman can knock down the ball . . . a quick recovery and immediate throw will turn the trick. Practice throwing from any position, since you must get rid of the ball as soon as possible."

Mike Schmidt on stopping hot smashes:

"Third base is the hot corner, that's for sure. You get the hardest hit and fastest ground balls there. Charge the ball and don't let it play you. You play *it*. Never be afraid of the ball. The ball won't hurt you."

Heinie Groh on playing the bunt:

"Play the line for the bunt. The pitcher will take care of bunts to your left. Furthermore, you will be facing first base when you pick up the ball, and that must be your aim. . . . Never play the ball one-handed unless it is absolutely necessary."

How to Play the Outfield

Joe DiMaggio on catching the ball:

"Make every catch in the best possible position from which to throw. I take fly balls with my hands above my head, left foot toward the plate, so as to save time making the throw. . . . If it is a bouncing ball, charge it in order to field it at the top of the hop, in good throwing position."

Making the throw:

"With a man on base, make up your mind in advance where you will throw, but be ready to react to any change in circumstances. The safest rule to follow is: Throw ahead of the runner. On throws to all bases, it is better to throw on one hop than on the fly. Also, low throws set up cutoff plays."

Tris Speaker on learning to judge fly balls:

"This is just about the most important thing to master. Go out to your ball grounds with one of your friends, station yourself in any of the three outfield positions, and have him stand at the home plate and hit 'fungoes' to you. Keep this up for weeks, until you can tell about how far a ball is going the instant you see it leave the bat."

Fielding ground balls:

"Outfields, as a rule, are not nearly as smooth as infields, and there is much more danger of bad bounds. The one rule you must live up to strictly is to get your body in front of a ball that is coming to you on the ground. . . . Stop a ground ball with your hands if possible, but have your body and your feet ready to help."

Where to play:

"An outfielder learns the habits of batters and 'lays' for them. Generally, if you are a left fielder, you are safe in playing close in for a lefthanded batter, and farther out for one who bats righthanded. If you are a right fielder, move in for a righthanded batter, and out for a lefthanded one."

UNOFFICIAL SINGLE-GAME RECORDS

Everyone needs goals. Big league ballplayers know all the major league baseball records, and they set out to break them when they play. Maybe you'd like to know some of the youth league records.

Little League, Babe Ruth League, Pony Baseball, and the American Amateur Baseball Congress (AABC) don't keep single-game records for players or for teams. But they do keep records for outstanding performances in a World Series game.

Those records are combined below and broken down by age group, so you can see where you stand: Under 10 (AABC/Willie Mays Division), 11–12 (Little League, Babe Ruth/Bambino Division, Pony/Bronco League, and AABC/Pee Wee Reese), and 13–15 (Babe Ruth Prep, Babe Ruth, Pony League and AABC/Sandy Koufax). All the leagues don't keep the same records, and some keep more than others. But they'll give you something to shoot for.

10 AND UNDER

Batting

Most Hits

5—D. Castro, Carolina, PR. AABC/Mays. 1987

Most Home Runs

2—P. Handley, Hapeville, GA. AABC/Mays. 1978
D. Moore, Topeka, KS, AABC/Mays. 1986

Most Runs Batted In

5—Held jointly by five players. Last to do it: C. Boyd, Owasso, OK. AABC/Mays. 1987; F. Llanos and E. Alamo, Carolina, PR. AABC/Mays. 1987

Most Doubles

3—M. Brinkley, Gresham Park, GA. AABC/Mays. 1977

Most Stolen Bases

7—J. Tover, Dallas, TX. AABC/Mays. 1979

Pitching

Most Strikeouts

13—Luis Lopez, Toa Baja, PR. AABC/Mays. 1984

No-Hitters—There have been seven. Last to do it: A. Martinez and J. Niebla, Paramount, CA. AABC/Mays. 1987

TEAM

Most Hits

23—Carolina, PR. AABC/Mays. 1987

Most Runs

25—Carolina, PR. AABC/Mays. 1987

Most Errors

12—Brooklyn, NY. AABC/Mays. 1980

Longest Game

9 innings—Carolina, PR.(5) vs. Paramount, CA (4). AABC/Mays. 1987

12 AND UNDER

Batting

Most Hits

5—Held jointly by eight players. Last to do it: DeShawn Serrano, Brooklyn, NY. Bambino. 1987

Most Home Runs

3—Held jointly by four players. Last to do it: Jorge Miranda, Bayamon, PR. AABC/Reese. 1986

Most Runs Batted In

9—Greg Burton, Huntington, W.VA. AABC/Reese. 1972

Most Runs

5—Larry Hooks, Gresham Park, GA, and Steve Gibralter, Dallas, TX. AABC/Reese. 1985; Arturo Figueroa, Levittown, PR. Bronco. 1987

Most Doubles

3—Pete Scanlan, Los Alamitos, CA. Bronco. 1983
Bill Shafer, Dallas, TX. AABC/Reese. 1985

Most Triples

1—Held jointly by many players.

Pitching
Most Strikeouts

21—Melvin Houston, Richmond, CA. Bronco. 1977
19—Jose Navedo, Bayamon, PR. AABC/Reese. 1983

Fewest Hits
Perfect game

Angel Macias, Monterrey, Mexico. Little League. 1957

No-Hitters—There have been twenty-nine. Last to do it: Alex Correa, Carolina, Puerto Rico. AABC/Reese. 1987
David Carino and Keola Esperas, Mililani Town, HI. Bronco. 1987

TEAM
Most Hits

26—Miami, FLA. AABC/Reese. 1987
21—Tainan City, Taiwan. Little League. 1973
19—Rockford, IL. Bronco. 1967

Most Home Runs

7—Hualian, Taiwan. Little League. 1980

Most Runs

28—Miami, FLA. AABC/Reese. 1987
27—Tainan City, Taiwan. Little League. 1973
25—Northern Phillipines. Bronco. 1984

Most Errors

13—Arakawa, Tokyo, Japan. Little League. 1965

Most Stolen Bases

15—Richmond, CA. Bronco. 1977

Longest Game

19 innings—San Pedro (Cabrillo Bay), CA 1 vs. Birmingham, AL 0. Bronco. 1969

13 TO 15
Hitting
Most Hits

6—Manuel Muniz, Caguas, PR. Pony. 1984
5—Held jointly by three players. Last to do it: Doug Smallwood, Frederick, MD. Babe Ruth. 1983
Jason Hammond, Dallas, TX. AABC/Reese. 1983

Most Consecutive Hits

9—Manuel Muniz, Caguas, PR. Pony. 1984

Most Home Runs

3—Tony Peeler, Kansas City, KS. AABC/Koufax. 1984
Vilato Marrero, Bayamon, PR. AABC/Koufax. 1984
James Hovorka, Maywood, IL. Pony. 1957
Joe Galatie, Bridgeport, CT. Pony. 1963

Most Home Runs, Inning

2—Osvaldo Sanchez, Caguas, PR. Pony. 1984

Most RBIs

7—Cale Gundy, Midwest City, OK. Pony. 1986

Most Runs

4—Held jointly by fifteen players.

Most Doubles

3—Held jointly by five players. Last to do it: Ryan Lau Hee, Maui, HI. Pony. 1983

Most Triples

1—Held jointly by many players.

Most Total Bases

12—Held jointly by three players. Last to do it: Bob Christensen, Houston (Kyle-Chapman), TX. Pony. 1979

Most Stolen Bases

6—Carlos Alvarez, Dorado, PR. AABC/Koufax. 1980

Pitching
Most Strikeouts

20—Mike Vefeades, Denver, CO. AABC/ Koufax. 1974
19—Carlos Rodriguez, Monterrey, Mexico. Pony 1972

Consecutive Strikeouts

10—Gene Morowski, Hamtramck, MI. Pony. 1958
Denny Phillips, Honolulu, HI. Pony.1971

Fewest Hits

There have been twenty-eight no-hitters. Last to do it: Jose Aponte, Caguas, PR. Pony. 1987
Clarence Johnson, New Orleans, LA. Babe Ruth/Prep. 1985

TEAM
Most Hits

22—Caguas, PR. Pony. 1984

Most Runs

26—Covina, CA. Pony. 1968

Most Runs, Inning

19—Houston (Kyle-Chapman), TX. Pony. 1979

Most Home Runs

5—Held jointly by five teams. Last to do it: Midwest City, OK. Pony. 1986

Home Runs, Inning

3—Held jointly by seven teams. Last to do it: Midwest City, OK. Pony. 1986

Most Stolen Bases

14—Oak Park, IL. Pony. 1981

Longest Game

16—Campbell-Moreland, CA (4) vs. Caguas, Puerto Rico (0). Pony. 1964
15—Terre Haute, IN (7) vs. Nashville, TN (4). Babe Ruth. 1967

BE GOOD TO YOUR BASEBALL EQUIPMENT . . .
and it will be good to you

How to Choose Your Baseball Glove

Baseball gloves come in so many shapes, sizes, and colors. How do you know which is right for you?

One thing is for sure: You can't judge a glove by its color. Big leaguer Tito Landrum used to have three gloves: one blue, one black, and one orange. The color didn't help him catch the ball any better.

But you can pick out a glove that will fit you . . . like a glove. And one that will help you field better. Here's what to look for.

Size of the glove

Gloves are measured from the heel (the part that covers your wrist) to the tip of the index finger. If you are eleven years old or under, try a glove that's about ten inches. If you are twelve and over, you can try moving up to an eleven- to twelve-inch model.

You might think that the bigger the glove, the easier it will be to catch the ball. But that's not always so. Dave Concepcion of the Cincinnati Reds wears a glove so small, he cannot fit his whole hand into it, just his fingers. He likes the flexibility.

If you are serious about becoming a good fielder, a smaller glove will help you get better. A smaller glove is easier to handle. You will be able to feel the ball in your glove, and find it more easily for quick throws.

Your field position

Gloves are made differently for different field positions.

Infielders use a smaller glove with a shallow pocket so that they can remove the ball quickly for throws. Joe Morgan, the great second baseman for the Astros, Reds, and Giants, used to wear a mitt so small, it was hardly bigger than a mitten.

Outfielders use bigger gloves to give them a longer reach. Big league pitchers like gloves with the webs closed up by strips of leather. That makes it easier for them to hide their grips of the ball.

Five easy steps to breaking in your glove

1. Pour a small amount of leather conditioner, mink oil, or glove oil onto a cloth and work it into the pocket, the back, and all around the glove.
2. Let the glove dry thoroughly—for a day, at least.
3. After it dries, play catch for fifteen minutes to stretch the pocket and mold the glove to your hand.
4. Work the glove in whenever you can. If you are watching TV, keep throwing a ball into the pocket.
5. Keep a ball in the pocket between uses (putting it under your mattress doesn't hurt).

Take care of your glove, and it will take care of you.

- Don't leave it lying around in damp places, like the garage, basement, or the trunk of your folks' car. Moisture will make your glove moldy.
- When you put it away for the season, keep a ball in the pocket to help the glove keep its shape.
- Give it another coat of oil to start next season.
- Remember: A baseball glove is a piece of leather. Treat it like you would treat your Sunday shoes.

How to Choose a Bat

The right bat is the one that feels comfortable for you. A bat that is too long or heavy won't make the ball go farther. A bat that has your favorite player's autograph on it, well . . . "That bat was picked by me because it felt comfortable to me," says Pete Rose. "I wasn't even thinking of you."

Check the chart on the next page (reprinted courtesy of Hillerich & Bradsby Co.) to see which length bat is best for your size. Bats sold in stores are marked only according to length, but you can figure one ounce per inch. A thirty-inch bat, for example, would weigh about thirty ounces.

Taking care of your wooden bat

- When it is new, or at the start of a season, you can bone your bat to give it a harder hitting surface. Take a soda bottle and slowly rub it along the grain of the bat. Boning compresses the grain of the wood and makes it tougher.
- After the season, rub a little linseed oil into your bat. It preserves the wood.
- Store your bat in a dry place. In a damp room, a bat will absorb moisture and pick up weight.
- Hit with the label up. Batting against the grain can cause your bat to break.
- Aluminum bats are easy to take care of. Don't use them to clean your spikes,

and don't throw them around. You don't want any dents in your bat.

How to Take Care of Your Baseball Cap

Okay, so you don't *have* to take care of your cap. But maybe you want to look good.

Bending the brim

When you buy a cap, the brim is flat. Take the brim in both hands, on either side of the visor, and gently roll it up and down, applying pressure with your thumbs. When you get a slight arch, stop. You never want to crease your brim.

Shaping the crown

When the cap is new, the little button on top of the crown sticks up. That doesn't look cool. So, using your fingers and palms, put a fold in the crown right by the eyelets. Don't make it a tight crease. Fold it just enough to make a peak.

Pocketing the cap

There is a trick to folding up the cap so it keeps its shape. At the point where the visor and the base of the crown meet, fold the crown down, right on top of the visor. Tuck in the back of the cap behind the peak of the crown to make it fit in your pocket. When you're ready to put it on again, just shake the cap back open.

Keeping it clean

If your cap gets dusty, just knock it against your leg a few times. If it gets really dirty, use an old toothbrush and some water. Never, ever, let your mom put it in the washing machine.

PLAYER'S WEIGHT	BATTER'S HEIGHT								
	3'–3'4"	3'5"–3'8"	3'9"–4'	4'1"–4'4"	4'5"–4'8"	4'9"–5'	5'1"–5'4"	5'5"–5'8"	5'9"–6'
Under 60 lbs.	26"	27"	28"	29"	29"	—	—	—	—
61–70	27"	27"	28"	29"	29"	30"	—	—	—
71–80	—	28"	28"	29"	30"	30"	31"	—	—
81–90	—	28"	29"	29"	30"	30"	31"	32"	—
91–100	—	28"	29"	30"	30"	31"	31"	32"	—
101–110	—	29"	29"	30"	30"	31"	31"	32"	—
111–120	—	29"	29"	30"	30"	31"	31"	32"	—
121–130	—	29"	30"	30"	30"	31"	32"	33"	33"
131–140	—	29"	30"	30"	31"	31"	32"	33"	34"
141–150	—	—	30"	30"	31"	31"	32"	33"	34"
151–160	—	—	30"	31"	31"	32"	32"	33"	34"
Over 160	—	—	—	31"	31"	32"	32"	33"	34"

TEAM _____

PLAYER	POS.	1	2	3	4	5	6	7	AB	R	H	BB	TB
									8	9	10	11	12
	R/H												

AMAZING STORIES

PITCHER	IP	H	R	ER	BB	SO

The Baltimore Orioles of the 1890s always had a few tricks up their sleeve—or someplace else.

Before a game, the O's outfielders would hide a few baseballs in the outfield grass. If a batter hit a ball past one of them for a sure extra-base hit, the outfielder would run to the nearest hidden ball and throw it back to hold the batter to a single.

One day, a batter hit a long ball between the O's left fielder and center fielder. The left fielder picked up a hidden ball and threw it back in. But the center fielder ran down the real ball and also made the play.

The trick had backfired. The umpire declared the Orioles losers of the game by forfeit.

CORNER OF FAME

Honus Wagner.

Some call the Flying Dutchman baseball's greatest all-around player ever. He hit over .300 17 years in a row and won 8 NL batting titles. He stole 722 bases in his career, leading the league five times. And he was a shovel-handed shortstop known for scooping up half the infield with a ground ball and throwing some of it along to first base. Wagner played for the Pirates around the turn of the century. He was an original Hall of Famer, elected in 1936.

20

As a young outfielder, you should learn to go back for a ball so that it is as easy for you as coming up or standing still, and then you won't be afraid to play as your judgment dictates.
—Tris Speaker

TEAM _____

PLAYER	POS.	1	2	3	4	5	6	7	AB 8	R 9	H 10	BB 11	TB 12
	R/H												

PITCHER	IP	H	R	ER	BB	SO

WHEN I WAS A KID

Dale Murphy, Outfield, Atlanta Braves. NL MVP, 1982, 1983.

"When I got my first Little League uniform, I didn't know how to put my socks on. I was nine years old when I played my first game. And I only had one hit that season. I thought *this* season was going to be like *that* one for a while."

Von Hayes, First base, Philadelphia. Led NL in doubles, runs in '86.

"I was pretty average. I was just a little guy playing shortstop. I didn't grow until college. I was not the best player in the league, but I always made All-Stars. . . . Our team used to win the area all the time. . . .

"I had no idea I'd be able to play in the big leagues. I just played for fun. I didn't think I had a chance."

JR. HALL OF FAME

The first Little Leaguer to play in the big leagues was Joey Jay. Joey helped pitch the Middletown, CT, Little League to the 1948 World Series. Five years later, he was a rookie with the Milwaukee Braves. Jay won 21 games for the Cincinnati Reds in 1961, and again in '62.

Q: What was the first big league stadium to have Astroturf instead of grass as its playing surface?
A: The Astrodome, in Houston

TEAM _____

PLAYER	POS.	1	2	3	4	5	6	7	AB / 8	R / 9	H / 10	BB / 11	TB / 12
		R / H											

AMAZING STORIES

Germany Schaefer, who played for Detroit in the early 1900s, was known to do a wild thing or two.

One day, with his teammate on third base and him on first, Schaefer called for a double steal. He stole second, but the catcher didn't throw, so his teammate had to hold third.

On the next pitch, Schaefer yelled, "Let's try it again!" and took off back to first base. Dumbfounded, the catcher again held the ball. Germany Schaefer became the first—and only—man in baseball to steal first base.

PITCHER	IP	H	R	ER	BB	SO

CORNER OF FAME

Pie Traynor.

Harold Joseph Traynor picked up the nickname Pie as a kid because of his regular visits to the bakery. He proved himself to be one of the greatest fielding third basemen of all time, with great range, for 17 seasons with the Pittsburgh Pirates in the '20s and '30s. But Pie could also hit. He drove in 100 runs 7 times and hit .300 10 times. Pie was widely respected as a fine team player too. He was elected to the Hall of Fame in 1948.

TEAM _____

PLAYER	POS.	1	2	3	4	5	6	7	AB	R	H	BB	TB
									8	9	10	11	12
	R / H												

PITCHER	IP	H	R	ER	BB	SO

> *Championship teams are not founded on bats. They're built on a backbone of catching, pitching, a second base combination, and a center fielder.*
> **—Carl Mays, Yankees pitcher**

TEAM_____

PLAYER	POS.	1	2	3	4	5	6	7	AB	R	H	BB	TB
									8	9	10	11	12
	R / H												

AMAZING STORIES

PITCHER	IP	H	R	ER	BB	SO

Jimmy St. Vrain was a 19-year-old pitcher for the Cubs in 1902. He was a lefthanded pitcher but a righthanded batter—and a terrible batter, at that. He never got a hit.

Jimmy pitched against Pittsburgh one game and struck out his first two times up. The next time up, his manager joked that maybe he should try batting left-handed too.

Jimmy took him seriously, went up to the plate, turned around, and faced the pitcher from the left-hand side. And he got a hit. He hit a slow ground ball to shortstop and ran like mad . . . to third base.

CORNER OF FAME

Roy Campanella.

In just ten years with the Brooklyn Dodgers, 1948–57, Campy was voted NL MVP three times. He was a team leader on the Dodgers, urging them on to 5 World Series. Roy slugged 30 or more home runs 4 times and drove in a league-high 142 runs in 1953. His career was cut short by an auto accident in 1958 that left him confined to a wheelchair. He was elected to the Hall of Fame in 1969.

DID YOU KNOW THAT . . .

The year they were immortalized in Franklin P. Adams's poem, 1908, the Cubs' Tinker to Evers to Chance combined for only sixteen double plays.

TEAM _____

PLAYER	POS.	1	2	3	4	5	6	7	AB	R	H	BB	TB
									8	9	10	11	12
	R/H												

WHEN I WAS A KID

PITCHER	IP	H	R	ER	BB	SO

Gary Carter, Catcher, New York Mets. Ten-time NL All-Star.

"When I was 12, I was a pitcher and went 13–0. I hit .666 and made the All-Star team. I also hit the longest home run ever in my league, over 300 feet. It was a great thrill."

Howard Johnson, Third base, New York Mets. 36 HRs, 32 SBs in 1987.

"I remember our team winning our Babe Ruth league when I was 13. We lost in the district tournament, but then in All-Stars, we won a couple of games. My most memorable experience was pitching in an All-Star tournament and losing.

"Our league was only allowed to have two 13-year-olds on the All-Star team, and I was one of them. I always wanted to be a professional ballplayer. That's the age when you can start to tell if you have what it takes."

JR. HALL OF FAME

In 1971, Lloyd McClendon led the Gary, Indiana, Little League to the title game of the World Series by hitting five home runs in five official at-bats. McClendon is now a catcher for the Cincinnati Reds.

The art of hitting is the art of getting your pitch to hit.

—Bobby Brown, former Yankee, now AL president

TEAM _____

PLAYER	POS.	1	2	3	4	5	6	7	AB	R	H	BB	TB
									8	9	10	11	12
	R/H												

AMAZING STORIES

PITCHER	IP	H	R	ER	BB	SO

One of the worst mental errors in baseball history took place in September 1908 in a game between the Giants and the Cubs.

They were tied for the league lead with only a week to go, and the score was tied 1–1 with two outs in the last of the ninth. With Giants runners on first and third, the next batter hit a single to center, driving in the winning run.

But as the crowd ran onto the field, the runner on first, 19-year-old Fred Merkle, sprinted for the clubhouse. He did not touch second base to complete the play.

The Cubs second baseman found the ball and tagged the bag. Merkle was forced out and the run did not score. The Cubs went on to win the game and the pennant.

CORNER OF FAME

Hank Greenberg.

Hank belted out 331 home runs in 13 big league seasons, mostly with Detroit. He led the league in round-trippers four times and hit 58 home runs in 1938. Greenberg drove in 170 runs in 1935, and 183 in 1937. In 1945, in the ninth inning of the last game, he hit a grand-slam home run to give the Tigers the pennant. He was elected to the Hall of Fame in 1956.

TEAM _____

PLAYER	POS.	1	2	3	4	5	6	7	AB / 8	R / 9	H / 10	BB / 11	TB / 12
	R / H												

PITCHER	IP	H	R	ER	BB	SO

WHEN I WAS A KID

Steve Garvey, First base, Dodgers and Padres, 1970–87. Holds NL record for consecutive games played.

"I had some embarrassing moments. When I played shortstop, I made a lot of errors. And some balls went right between my legs.

"Once in a while I'd pitch. I remember a tournament game we were in. It went nine innings. I pitched all nine and struck out twenty. I allowed only one hit. And we lost the game.

"That was the first time I ever extended myself physically. I was 12 years old. I came to realize that was good for me. That experience carried over in the major leagues for me."

JR. HALL OF FAME

In the 1980 World Series, Gary Sheffield of Tampa, Florida starred for the Belmont Heights Little League All-Star team. He caught, and played first base. In the three games, Gary had seven hits, with four doubles, a home run, nine RBIs and eight runs scored. But Tampa lost to Taiwan in the title game.

Today, Gary is a promising prospect in the Milwaukee Brewers minor league system. He is also Dwight Gooden's nephew.

Q: The American League introduced the designated hitter in 1973. Who was the first DH to bat in a game?
A: Rom Blomberg of the N.Y. Yankees

TEAM _____

PLAYER	POS.	1	2	3	4	5	6	7	AB	R	H	BB	TB
									8	9	10	11	12
	R / H												

AMAZING STORIES

PITCHER	IP	H	R	ER	BB	SO

In the fifth inning of Game Four of the 1920 World Series, Cleveland second sacker Bill Wambsganss became a household name.

The Dodgers had men on first and third, nobody out. The next batter hit a line drive, just to Wambsganss's right and a little over his head. Bill ran and jumped, and snagged the ball. One out. His momentum carried him to second base. The Dodger baserunner was well on his way to third, so Wambsganss just stepped on the bag. Two outs. He turned around to see the Dodger runner from first standing right in front of him. Tag play. Three outs.

Bill Wambsganss, in a World Series game, had made an unassisted triple play.

CORNER OF FAME

Jackie Robinson.

Jackie Robinson was the first black man to play in the major leagues in the twentieth century. Robinson was a fierce competitor and an exciting baserunner. He led the NL in stolen bases twice, and piled up 19 steals of home. His best year at the plate was 1949, when he hit .342 with 124 RBIs and was named MVP. In ten seasons, he helped the Dodgers win six pennants. He was elected to the Hall of Fame in 1962.

TEAM _____

PLAYER	POS.	1	2	3	4	5	6	7	AB	R	H	BB	TB
									8	9	10	11	12
	R / H												

WHEN HE WAS A KID

PITCHER	IP	H	R	ER	BB	SO

Steve Carlton, Pitcher, St. Louis, Philadelphia, and others. 329 wins, 4,131 strikeouts, four Cy Young awards.

"Through age 11, Steve—who always was a shy boy—just played ball on the street. Our house was surrounded by trees. The only way to throw a ball was up.

"Then a boy moved across the street from us. He had played Little League. He was just finishing up. Steve got acquainted with him. The next year Steve decided he wanted to play Little League.

"I got Steve signed up. He said he wanted to pitch or play first base. He became a pitcher. The first two games he pitched were no-hitters."

—Joe Carlton,
Steve's dad

JR. HALL OF FAME

Former big league pitcher Mickey Lolich still holds the Babe Ruth World Series record for most innings pitched in a game.

Lolich pitched for his Portland, OR, team in 1955. He set a Series record by hurling twelve innings in a game. Lolich won 217 games in his career, 207 for the Tigers, and was the MVP of the 1968 World Series.

> *I got three pitches: my change; my change off my change; and my change off my change off my change.*
>
> *—Preacher Roe*

TEAM _____

PLAYER	POS.	1	2	3	4	5	6	7	AB	R	H	BB	TB
									8	9	10	11	12
R/H													

AMAZING STORIES

PITCHER	IP	H	R	ER	BB	SO

Rube Waddell was one of the greatest pitchers in the game—certainly the funniest.

One time, his Pittsburgh club was playing an exhibition game on Easter Sunday against a team in Memphis. They were well ahead in the bottom of the ninth. Then someone in the stands threw an egg that hit Rube right on the head.

Rube decided to show that crowd a thing or two. He called in his outfielders and pitched the bottom of the ninth with just his infield behind him.

And he struck out the side.

CORNER OF FAME

Jimmie Foxx.

Old Double-X ranked up there with Babe Ruth during his playing days from 1925 to 1945. The Philadelphia A's and Boston Red Sox first baseman hit 534 home runs. Foxx hit 50 or more home runs twice, and 48 another time. He hit 58 in 1932, and might have tied Ruth's record of 60, but rain washed out two of his homers. He was a two-time AL MVP and won the Triple Crown in 1933. Foxx used to snip off his uniform sleeves to show his muscles. He was elected to the Hall of Fame in 1951.

DID YOU KNOW THAT . . .

The Cy in Cy Young, the winningest pitcher of all time with 511 victories, stands for cyclone. He was born Denton True Young.

TEAM _____

PLAYER	POS.	1	2	3	4	5	6	7	AB	R	H	BB	TB
									8	9	10	11	12
	R/H												

WHEN I WAS A KID

Darryl Strawberry, Outfield, New York Mets. 39 HRs and 36 SBs in 1987.

"Those were the great days. You didn't have to deal with pressure. Everyone you played with was as young as you were, so you got to enjoy the baseball and do your best as a team. I have some great memories. I remember some great games and some great victories, especially when our team went to Seattle for the regional championships.

"I thought everyone had just as much talent as I did. You didn't compete with each other at that time. I never set any records in

PITCHER	IP	H	R	ER	BB	SO

Babe Ruth. I was just in the right place at the right time."

JR. HALL OF FAME

Some of the Most Outstanding Players of Babe Ruth World Series went on to play in the major leagues:

• Mickey Lolich (Portland, OR), 1956.

• Willie Montanez (Puerto Nueva, Puerto Rico), 1963.

• Ken Brett (El Segundo, CA), 1964.

• Scott McGregor (El Segundo, CA), 1969.

31

> *You would be amazed how many important outs you can get by working the count down to where the hitter is sure you're going to throw to his weakness and then throw to his strength instead.*
> —*Whitey Ford*

Q: In 1984, Dwight Gooden set a big league rookie record by striking out 276 batters. Who held the old NL record?
A: Hall of Famer Grover Alexander

TEAM _____

PLAYER	POS.	1	2	3	4	5	6	7	AB	R	H	BB	TB
									8	9	10	11	12
	R / H												

AMAZING STORIES

With the Chicago fans jeering him in the fifth inning of the third game of the 1932 World Series, Babe Ruth settled into the batter's box and awaited pitcher Charlie Root's delivery.

Strike one. Ruth beat the umpire to the call, raising a finger into the air. The crowd yelled louder.

Strike two. Ruth raised two fingers. The crowd went crazy.

Ruth smiled and pointed toward the flagpole in center field. And on the next pitch, he hit the ball right there for a home run. You could smell the crowd burning as the Babe circled the bases in peaceful silence.

PITCHER	IP	H	R	ER	BB	SO

CORNER OF FAME

Christy Mathewson.

Matty the Great was a college man and one of the gentlemen of the game. He had been class president at Bucknell. But he also was one of baseball's great pitchers. Hurling his famous fadeaway pitch for the New York Giants in the early years of the 1900s, Matty won 20 games as a rookie, then went on to have four 30-win seasons, including 37 in 1908, a modern NL record. An original Hall of Famer, he was elected in 1936.

The one thing you want to remember when catching a ground ball is to keep your glove as low as you can get it. I've seen infielders come up with a handful of dirt after fielding a grounder.
—Pete Rose

TEAM _____

PLAYER	POS.	1	2	3	4	5	6	7	AB	R	H	BB	TB
									8	9	10	11	12
	R / H												

PITCHER	IP	H	R	ER	BB	SO

WHEN I WAS A KID

Roger McDowell, Pitcher, New York Mets. 64 saves in first three seasons.

"I pretty much remember everything about that time in my life. Our coach formed a team of select players and we compiled a 97–10 record. We were by far the best team in the area. We traveled and we got to take a week off from school. It was like we supported ourselves, and that was the best part of it. That and knowing about winning.

"I didn't excel then. I was physically small and I was not a power pitcher. I made a lot of sacrifices to play Babe Ruth. We practiced every day in the summer. It's gratifying to look back now and know it all paid off."

JR. HALL OF FAME

• Ken Brett, the brother of George Brett and a former big league pitcher himself, threw a no-hitter in the 1964 Babe Ruth World Series.

• Rick Wise, who would later pitch for Philadelphia and St. Louis, got his first taste of stardom when he hurled a no-hitter for Portland, OR, in the 1961 Babe Ruth World Series.

Q: What do Ted Williams's .406 batting average and Joe DiMaggio's 56-game hitting streak have in common?
A: Both happened in 1941

TEAM _____

PLAYER	POS.	1	2	3	4	5	6	7	AB	R	H	BB	TB
									8	9	10	11	12
	R/H												

AMAZING STORIES

In 1934, New York Giants' pitcher Carl Hubbell had the privilege of starting the All-Star Game before a crowd of 48,000 in his home park, the Polo Grounds.

But in the first inning, two men reached base with no out, and Hubbell had to face the most fearsome group of sluggers ever assembled. The next five hitters were Babe Ruth, Lou Gehrig, Jimmie Foxx, Al Simmons, and Joe Cronin, all future Hall of Famers.

Hubbell, who threw a mean screwball, turned up the gas. He struck out Ruth, Gerhrig, and Foxx on nine pitches, ending the first inning. Then he fanned Simmons and Cronin on six straight strikes to start the second.

Alas, despite Hubbell's great start, the NL lost the game to the AL, 9–7.

CORNER OF FAME

Hank Aaron.

You probably already know about his 755 home runs that broke Babe Ruth's longtime record. But Hammerin' Hank also holds the career record for most RBI's, is second all-time in runs and at-bats, and third in hits and games played. In 23 big league seasons, Aaron averaged .305, with 33 home runs and 100 RBIs. Those are Hall of Fame numbers. He was elected in 1982.

PITCHER	IP	H	R	ER	BB	SO

34

Always keep in mind the number of outs, which bases are occupied, and the score. Think out each play before it happens. If you boot the ball, think where you're going to throw it even before you pick it up, so no time is lost.

—Honus Wagner

TEAM _____

PLAYER	POS.	1	2	3	4	5	6	7	AB	R	H	BB	TB
									8	9	10	11	12
	R / H												

PITCHER	IP	H	R	ER	BB	SO

WHEN I WAS A KID

Mike Scioscia, L.A. Dodgers' regular catcher since 1985. Scioscia is also one of the best in baseball at blocking the plate and he led the league in putouts in 1987.

"I liked the traveling. I started playing Babe Ruth when I was 13, and I played until I was 18, in Senior Babe Ruth. It was a much better league than the other local leagues because of the traveling in tournaments.

"It was great exposure and great experience. The friendships I made there are going to last longer than the ones I made as a professional.

"I missed a year in Senior Babe Ruth because I was drafted by the Dodgers. I missed being in the league that year, believe it or not, because my friends were playing.

"When I played in Babe Ruth, I thought a lot of kids were as talented or better than me. I was just fortunate that the scouts saw something in me."

JR. HALL OF FAME

Steve Kemp still holds the record for most hits in a Pony League World Series, with 11. Steve, who played for Aracadia, CA, collected 11 hits in the 1969 Series. Steve Kemp played 10 years in the big leagues and batted .278 lifetime.

I became a good pitcher when I stopped trying to make them miss the ball and started trying to make them hit it.

—Sandy Koufax

TEAM _____

PLAYER	POS.	1	2	3	4	5	6	7	AB	R	H	BB	TB
									8	9	10	11	12
	R/H												

AMAZING STORIES

PITCHER	IP	H	R	ER	BB	SO

On May 2, 1917, pitchers Fred Toney of Cincinnati and Hippo Vaughn of the Cubs locked horns in the only double no-hit game in baseball history.

Inning after inning, Toney and Vaughn set down the opposing batters with hardly a whimper. Each pitcher issued but two walks.

The ninth inning came and went. Still no score. Then, in the top of the tenth, the Reds hit a single off Vaughn. An error sent the runner to third. And he scored on a slow roller.

Toney set down the Cubs in order in the bottom of the tenth to win the battle of the no-hitters.

CORNER OF FAME

Lou Brock.

The St. Louis Cardinal speedster is the greatest base stealer in baseball history. Brock, who started his career with the Cubs, stole a record 938 bases over his career. He led the league in thefts eight times in a nine-year stretch, topping it off with 118 steals, an NL record, in 1974. Brock was also an outstanding hitter, collecting 3,023 over his career. He was elected to the Hall of Fame in 1985.

I watch the pitcher's hand as the ball leaves it. I follow it to the hitter and keep my eyes on it when it comes off the bat. This helps me get a jump on the ball.

—**Ozzie Smith**

TEAM _____

PLAYER	POS.	1	2	3	4	5	6	7	AB	R	H	BB	TB
									8	9	10	11	12
		R / H											

PITCHER	IP	H	R	ER	BB	SO

WHEN I WAS A KID

Carl Yastrzemski, Outfield, Boston, 1961–83. Triple Crown (1967), 452 home runs.

"I'd pitch nine innings a week and strike out eighteen or nineteen batters. I threw this big round-house curveball. It would seem to be heading for a spot behind the batter's back. Then it would break over the plate and really scare him."

When Carl was 11 and 12 years old, he pitched Little League ball in his hometown of Bridgehampton, NY. He was a rising star in what was then isolated farm country on the eastern end of Long Island. But like every Little Leaguer's nightmare, Carl hurt his arm from throwing too many curveballs. By the time of his sophomore year of high school, the arm had become a real problem.

"I couldn't even pick up a ball that year. I was very fortunate that my arm came back later on. Of course, a sore arm never hurt my hitting."

Carl had always been a good hitter. So he gave up pitching and moved to the outfield. He also concentrated more on his batting. As a result, he hit better than .500 in high school.

Soon all the big league scouts were making the long trip out to Bridgehampton.

Q: Who was baseball's all-time home run king before Babe Ruth?
A: Roger Connor (136 career homers)

TEAM _____

| PLAYER | POS. | 1 | 2 | 3 | 4 | 5 | 6 | 7 | AB | R | H | BB | TB |
									8	9	10	11	12
	R / H												

AMAZING STORIES

PITCHER	IP	H	R	ER	BB	SO

Dizzy Dean, the Hall of Fame pitcher for the Cardinals in the 1930s, had a way of making bold predictions—and delivering.

One time, Dizzy told some kids in a hospital that he would strike out the Giants' best hitter, Bill Terry with the bases loaded.

Sure enough, the next day, in the ninth inning, the Giants put two men on base with two out, and the on-deck batter was Terry. Even though he was up only one run, Dean intentionally walked the batter to bring up Terry with the bases loaded. Then he struck him out on three pitches.

As Dizzy himself said, "If you can do it, it ain't bragging."

CORNER OF FAME

George Sisler.

Gorgeous George was the finest fielding first sacker of his day. He also was one of the most feared hitters. Sisler batted .407 in 1920 and .420 in 1922. In 1920, he collected 257 hits, still a big league record. Sisler batted over .300 in 13 of his 15 big league seasons. He was a graduate of Michigan and joined the St. Louis Browns as a pitcher. He later played for the Braves. He was elected to the Hall in 1939.

38

TEAM _____

PLAYER	POS.	1	2	3	4	5	6	7	AB	R	H	BB	TB
									8	9	10	11	12
	R/H												

WHEN I WAS A KID

PITCHER	IP	H	R	ER	BB	SO

Al Lopez, Catcher/Manager. After nineteen-year playing career, led Indians to pennant in 1954, and White Sox to flag in '59.

"In 1925, a team of big leaguers came barnstorming through Tampa right after the World Series, planning on playing each other or playing against a local pickup team. When they got to Tampa, they thought it might be a good idea to get one of the local kids to play with them, to attract some customers. I was asked. . . .

" 'Great,' I said. 'Who's pitching?'

" 'Walter Johnson,' they said.

"This was a little more than I'd expected. . . . Johnson was very nice. Just before we went out to warm up, he came over to me and said, 'Look, I'm not going to really let out. I'm going to bear down on just two fellows—Ike Boone and Jack Fournier. They hit me pretty good. . . . You be ready when they come up.

"He pitched just five innings that day, so he faced those guys twice each, and he struck them out twice each. Johnson must have been around 38 then . . . but he could still fire it when he wanted to. . . .

"After it was over, he told somebody, 'That boy did real well back there. Handled himself fine.' You can bet that made me feel good."

39

It ain't nothin' till I call it.
—Bill Klem, Hall of Fame umpire

TEAM _____

PLAYER	POS.	1	2	3	4	5	6	7	AB	R	H	BB	TB
									8	9	10	11	12
	R/H												

AMAZING STORIES

PITCHER	IP	H	R	ER	BB	SO

Most pitchers go through an entire career without tossing a no-hitter. In all of baseball history, only one man has ever pitched no-hitters back to back.

Johnny Vander Meer of the Cincinnati Reds did the impossible over five days in June 1938. First, he shut down Boston at his home field on June 11. He faced only twenty-eight men, giving up three walks.

And he kept on going. Pitching under the lights in the first night game at Brooklyn's Ebbets Field, Vander Meer was again unhittable.

He even spiced up the drama in the ninth inning, loading the bases before fanning the final batter. He did walk eight men, but then, nobody's perfect.

CORNER OF FAME

Napoleon Lajoie.

"Larry" Lajoie was a great second baseman for Philadelphia and Cleveland at the turn of the century. He batted over .350 ten times. When the American League was formed in 1901, Lajoie jumped from the Philadelphia Phillies to the Philadelphia Athletics and hit .422 to lead the league, the first of his three batting titles. That season he also led the league in home runs, and RBI's. He was elected to the Hall of Fame in 1937.

TEAM _____

PLAYER	POS.	1	2	3	4	5	6	7	AB	R	H	BB	TB
									8	9	10	11	12
	R / H												

WHEN I WAS A KID

PITCHER	IP	H	R	ER	BB	SO

Tommy John, Pitcher, White Sox, Dodgers, Yankees, and others. Three-time 20-game winner.

"I guess I learned the importance of fundamentals back in Little League. My dad was the manager of our team, which was sponsored by the Art Compton Cleaners in Terre Haute, Indiana. We learned that it was fun to do things the right way. No fooling around.

"For instance, Dad used to lay the shin guards on the infield about ten feet up each baseline, and we would practice bunting at those shin guards. Anytime a bunter would hit one of the guards, he'd get an ice-cream cone.

"Another thing I learned when I was ten years old was the proper way to throw a curve. The Philadelphia Phillies had a minor league farm team in Terre Haute. They were managed by Bennie Bengough.

"My dad asked Bengough to look at my curve, and he helped me learn the right way to snap it off.

Most kids never learn the proper snap, so they hurt their arms. I threw only three or four a game in Little League, but they were the right curves and they didn't bother me."

TEAM _____

PLAYER	POS.	1	2	3	4	5	6	7	AB	R	H	BB	TB
									8	9	10	11	12
	R / H												

PITCHER	IP	H	R	ER	BB	SO

AMAZING STORIES

Joe DiMaggio's 56-game hitting streak in 1941 is considered one of the greatest feats in any sport.

The streak began on May 15 and lasted until July 17. In that time DiMaggio batted .408, with 16 doubles, 4 triples, and 15 home runs.

The day the streak ended, the Yankee Clipper came up in his last at-bat to face Cleveland knuckleballer Jim Bagby. DiMaggio hit a hard grounder up the middle that looked like a sure hit. But the ball took a funny bounce, right up to Hall of Fame shortstop Lou Boudreau, who turned it into a double play.

CORNER OF FAME

Satchel Paige.
Leroy "Satchel" Paige was a great pitcher and a great showman. He was the star of the Negro Leagues in the 1930s and '40s. Paige won 31 games for the Pittsburgh Crawfords in 1933, with 16 shutouts. He once struck out 21 major leaguers in an exhibition game. Satch joined Bill Veeck's Cleveland Indians as a 42-year-old rookie in 1948, and helped them win a pennant. Paige pitched again for Veeck in St. Louis, and came back for a three-inning appearance for the Kansas City A's in 1965 at age 59. He was elected to the Hall of Fame in 1971.

TEAM _____

PLAYER	POS.	1	2	3	4	5	6	7	AB	R	H	BB	TB
									8	9	10	11	12
	R / H												

PITCHER	IP	H	R	ER	BB	SO

WHEN I WAS A KID

Bill Freehan, Catcher, Detroit, 1961–76. Hit 24 HRs for '68 World Champs, Gold Glove winner.

"I never intended to be a catcher. Back in Little League, I was a shortstop. One day, a kid didn't show up and I was asked to catch. The coach was a cop, so I did what he said."

Billy was a natural behind the plate. He made the Little League All-Star team in his hometown of Royal Oak, Michigan. And during Freehan's four years with the Royal Oak Tool Company team, they won the league title three times.

"I know I learned more about baseball than most kids my age."

Freehan always enjoyed the strategy of pitching. And in high school, he took it up whenever he wasn't catching. He wasn't big league material on the mound, but he did learn a lot about how a pitcher works.

When he reached the big leagues as a catcher, his knowledge of how to handle pitchers was well respected among managers and coaches.

"The biggest kick I got was to go out to the mound during a game and straighten out a guy who was having trouble. If I could do it, then I was more valuable to the team than if I hit four for five."

TEAM _____

PLAYER	POS.	1	2	3	4	5	6	7	AB	R	H	BB	TB
									8	9	10	11	12
		R/H											

AMAZING STORIES

PITCHER	IP	H	R	ER	BB	SO

With many stars away in the armed forces during World War II, baseball was in need of players who might not have made it at another time. That meant an opportunity for Pete Gray.

Pete Gray was a one-armed outfielder who played for Bill Veeck's St. Louis Browns in 1945.

Gray had lost his arm when he was a boy, but he loved baseball. He learned to hit with one arm, and to catch and throw by flipping the ball into the air while he freed his hand of his glove to throw.

Pete had hit .333 in the minors, but he didn't play much in St. Louis. He lost his spot on the team when the war ended and the stars came home. But he got a chance to play big league ball.

CORNER OF FAME

Bob Lemon.

Lem won 20 or more games seven times in nine years for the Cleveland Indians and helped pitch them to pennants in 1948 and 1954. He started out as an infielder/outfielder and didn't become a big league pitcher until age 26. In just thirteen seasons, the crafty righthander won 207 games, including a no-hitter against Detroit in 1948. He was elected to the Hall of Fame in 1976.

Do not try to slide away from every baseman. There are some who will expect you to slide away from them; they will be prepared to tag you. Never do what a man expects you to do; try to do the opposite.

—Ty Cobb

TEAM _____

PLAYER	POS.	1	2	3	4	5	6	7	AB	R	H	BB	TB
									8	9	10	11	12
	R / H												

WHEN I WAS A KID

PITCHER	IP	H	R	ER	BB	SO

Ted Williams, Outfield, Red Sox, 1939–42, 1946–60. Two Triple Crowns. 522 HRs, .344 BA. Elected to Hall of Fame, 1966.

"I pitched when I was a kid because there was more action there, and I played first base and outfield. I was on the junior-high team, Horace Mann Junior High, and then the American Legion Post team, and the sandlot teams in the summer. Good sandlot teams. We challenged the Navy teams off the Lexington and the Saratoga, which were tied up in San Diego harbor. . . .

"I had a picture of Babe Ruth on my wall, but my mother always made more of that than I did. Somebody would ask her, 'Who was Ted's idol?' and she'd tell them Babe Ruth. . . . I followed the big leagues, but I wasn't all the time digging into the sports pages, memorizing the averages, listening to games on the radio. I was out doing it. . . .

"I never thought I was the best player around. Roy Engle, who lived down the street, was better than I was, and a kid named Ted Gray. Both were bigger, stronger guys. I wasn't a home run hitter then. I wasn't strong enough—the biggest bag of bones you ever saw. But I could dream."

45

TEAM _____

PLAYER	POS.	1	2	3	4	5	6	7	AB	R	H	BB	TB
									8	9	10	11	12
R / H													

PITCHER	IP	H	R	ER	BB	SO

AMAZING STORIES

Don Larsen was not a great pitcher. But he pitched what was probably the greatest game in baseball history.

In 1955, Larsen hurled a perfect game for the Yankees as they beat the Dodgers in the fifth game of the World Series. He was helped by a home run by Mickey Mantle, and by some great defensive play.

In the second inning, Jackie Robinson hit a line drive off the third baseman's mitt, but shortstop Gil McDougald threw him out at first. In the fifth inning, Gil Hodges hit a line drive to left center. But Mantle ran it down. Later, Sandy Amoros hit a long fly ball that just curved foul.

Larsen threw only 97 pitches that day. But they were the right ones.

CORNER OF FAME

Rogers Hornsby.

The Rajah was considered the game's greatest righthanded hitter and second baseman. He played for twenty-three years (from 1915 to 1937), mostly with the Cardinals, Browns, and Cubs. Hornsby won six batting crowns. His .424 in 1924 is a twentieth-century major league mark. Twice he led the league in home runs and RBIs too. As a player-manager, he led the 1926 Cardinals to their first World Championship. He was elected to the Hall of Fame in 1942.

TEAM _____

PLAYER	POS.	1	2	3	4	5	6	7	AB	R	H	BB	TB
									8	9	10	11	12
	R / H												

PITCHER	IP	H	R	ER	BB	SO

WHEN I WAS A KID

Willie Mays, Outfield, Giants, Mets, 1951–72. Two-time NL MVP, 660 HRs, 11 Gold Gloves. Hall of Fame, 1979.

"My father was a very good baseball player. He was quick, really quick, and got the nickname Kitty Cat. He played in Birmingham's Industrial League, which often attracted six thousand fans a game. He took me to as many games as he could, and I was allowed to sit on the bench next to the grown-ups.

"There, I'd hear them discuss strategy—how you'd play a right-handed pull hitter who was batting against a guy with a slow curve. Or how big a lead you could afford to take off first when you had a southpaw with a quick delivery on the mound.

"So baseball really came naturally to me, more so than to most other kids. My father never pushed me into becoming a baseball player. He just exposed me to it, and it happened all by itself from there. . . .

"When I try to remember events as a kid, in my memories somehow a ball always winds up in my hands. I was forever hitting one or throwing one or catching one. Playing ball was an obsession."

Q: The first World Series was held in 1903. What two teams played?
A: Pittsburgh Pirates and Boston Red Sox

TEAM _____

PLAYER	POS.	1	2	3	4	5	6	7	AB	R	H	BB	TB
									8	9	10	11	12
		R / H											

PITCHER	IP	H	R	ER	BB	SO

AMAZING STORIES

Ted Williams was batting .3996 going into the last day of the 1941 season. If that number were rounded off, Williams would go into the record books as a .400 hitter. His manager asked him if he wanted to sit out the doubleheader that day just to play it safe.

But Williams would have none of that. He made four hits in the first game, and two in the second. His final average: .406.

Nineteen years later, Williams came up for the last at-bat of his career. He had started the game wanting to hit one final home run. Now was his last chance. He crushed the ball for a home run, rounded the bases, and disappeared into the clubhouse, forever.

CORNER OF FAME

Josh Gibson.

Josh Gibson was a power-hitting catcher who slugged almost 800 home runs in Negro League and independent baseball during his seventeen-year career. Josh hit 75 home runs in 1931 at the age of 19. In the mid-1940s, he hit three home runs in one game in Washington's Griffith Stadium. He died of a brain tumor at age 35. He was elected to the Hall of Fame in 1972.

TEAM _____

PLAYER	POS.	1	2	3	4	5	6	7	AB	R	H	BB	TB
									8	9	10	11	12
	R / H												

PITCHER	IP	H	R	ER	BB	SO

WHEN I WAS A KID

Don Mattingly, First base, N.Y. Yankees. AL MVP 1985. Record 6 grand slams, 1987.

"I played Babe Ruth Baseball when I was 13 and 14, and then, at 15, I played American Legion. The level of competition was good, but you don't know any different at that time because that's all you've seen."

Don doesn't remember how far his 13-year-old All-Star team advanced, but he seems to recall that they lost at the state level.

"There were changes from league to league. You learned by seeing better competition. The distance from the mound was different, the plate was different, the bases were different. The features were different, and so you learned that way.

"My coaches gave me a lot of constructive criticism. It really helped me a lot. At the time I could handle it. When you're younger, you get embarrassed more easily in front of people.

"My coaches made me work harder and harder to become better and better. I had that type of push from behind, but it wasn't on an individual basis. I was one of a group being pushed. And that's how it should be."

Q: Only one pitcher in baseball history ever pitched a no-hitter in an opening day game. Who did it?
A: Bob Feller

TEAM _____

PLAYER	POS.	1	2	3	4	5	6	7	AB	R	H	BB	TB
									8	9	10	11	12
		R / H											

AMAZING STORIES

PITCHER	IP	H	R	ER	BB	SO

It was the seventh game of the World Series, tie score, the bottom of the ninth. . .

Although the 1960 Series was knotted at three games apiece, it seemed to favor the Yankees, who had walloped the Pirates 16–3, 10–0, and 12–0 in their victories.

But the Pirates kept hanging tough, even when the Yankees built a 7–4 lead in the eighth inning of the seventh game.

The Bucs rallied to score five times in the bottom of the eighth to go ahead. But the Yanks came right back. So with the score tied 9–9 in the bottom of the ninth of the seventh game of the World Se- ries, up stepped Pirate second baseman Bill Mazeroski.

You guessed it. Home run. The Pirates won the Series.

CORNER OF FAME

Walter Johnson.

The Big Train pitched in the early 1900s for the Washington Senators. Although the Senators were bad, Johnson was one of the all-time greats, winning 416 games and striking out 3,508 batters with a great fastball and sweeping sidearm delivery. Johnson pitched a record 110 shutouts. He was an original member of the Hall of Fame, elected in 1936.

TEAM _____

PLAYER	POS.	1	2	3	4	5	6	7	AB	R	H	BB	TB
									8	9	10	11	12
	R/H												

PITCHER	IP	H	R	ER	BB	SO

WHEN I WAS A KID

Joe Cronin, Shortstop, Washington, Red Sox, and others. 1926–45. Seven-time All-Star, AL MVP, 1930. Hall of Fame, 1956.

"Since I was seven years old, I guess I always wanted to be a ballplayer. It was in my blood. Used to nip trucks to get to the ballpark.

"Funny thing about that. I learned that you could get into Recreation Park—that's where the Seals played—if you went down there early and helped the man who was in charge of the turnstiles. So I went down one day and helped this fellow set up, and sure enough, he let me in.

"I was the first person in the ballpark, and I went out to the bleachers to watch the players warm up. Four Oakland players started playing pepper out behind second base, hitting the ball toward where I was sitting in center field.

"Well, the ball got by all three of the fielders, and in my anxiety to assist, I jumped over the fence, got the ball, and rolled it back to them. Next thing I knew this cop was throwing me out of the ballpark.

"After dreaming all night long about how I was gonna get in free, I got myself kicked out before the game even started.

"A few years later, I came into the ballpark as a member of the Pittsburgh Pirates."

Q: Which pitcher holds the all-time record for most losses in a career?
A: Cy Young, who had 313 losses to go with his record 511 wins.

TEAM _____

PLAYER	POS.	1	2	3	4	5	6	7	AB	R	H	BB	TB
									8	9	10	11	12
	R/H												

AMAZING STORIES

PITCHER	IP	H	R	ER	BB	SO

Tony Cloninger of the 1966 Atlanta Braves had the best day a pitcher has ever had with the bat.

On July 3, he faced the Giants at Candlestick Park. Before he had a chance to pitch, he was at the plate, with the bases loaded, his team already up three home runs. Cloninger took a big swing and sent the ball over 400 feet for a grand-slam home run.

When he came to bat in the fourth, Cloninger also found the bases loaded. Another big swing and another grand slam. He later singled home another run.

Two grand slams, 9 RBIs, and a 17–3 victory. Not a bad day for a pitcher.

CORNER OF FAME

Tris Speaker.

One of the all-time great outfielders, The Grey Eagle patrolled Cleveland from 1907 to 1928. He was famous for playing shallow and throwing out more runners than anyone in history. He had 449 assists, twice dropping 35 pigeons in a season. Speaker could hit too. His lifetime average was .344. As a manager in 1920, he led Cleveland to its first World Championship. He was elected to the Hall of Fame in 1937.

You must hold the bat loosely in order to make a good bunt. Most bunts are made simply by letting the ball hit the bat.

—Enos Slaughter

TEAM _____

PLAYER	POS.	1	2	3	4	5	6	7	AB	R	H	BB	TB
									8	9	10	11	12
	R/H												

WHEN I WAS A KID

PITCHER	IP	H	R	ER	BB	SO

Sandy Koufax, Pitcher, Dodgers, 1955–66. Won 25 or more games three times. Pitched four no-hitters in four years. Hall of Fame, 1972.

"In my early years [in the Borough Park section of Brooklyn] I was a street kid—'street' meaning the schoolyard, the playground, the parks, the beaches, the community centers. I went where the games were.

"The buildings in our neighborhood were single- and double-story wooden houses, with what we called 'stoops' in Brooklyn, although they seem to be called porches everyplace else. Leading up to the stoops were three or four steps on which the younger kids would play stoopball—throwing the ball against the steps until somebody's mother came and kicked you away.

"From stoopball you graduated into stickball and punchball. . . . The bases were probably the fender of a car on one side of the street and a hydrant on the other, with a sewer cover for second base. The ball, being fairly soft, could not be hit for any great distance, and if you hit one that covered two sewers, you were a man of distinction."

BATTING TOTALS

PLAYER	AB	R	H	BB	HR	RBI	TB	SB	BA	OBA	SLG	PRO	GWRBI

AMAZING STORIES

It was a hot pennant race that summer of 1951, when the Giants came from way back to finish the season in a tie with the Dodgers. They would have to have a best two-out-of-three playoff to determine the NL champion.

The Giants won the first game, and the Dodgers the second. So now the pennant would be decided by a single game at the Polo Grounds.

With their ace righthander Don Newcombe looking unbeatable, the Dodgers went into the ninth with a 4–1 lead and the pennant seemingly locked up.

But then the Giants rallied, and soon it was 4–2, with two runners in scoring position. Out went Newcombe. In came Ralph Branca to pitch for the Dodgers. Up came Bobby Thomson to bat.

The next sound anyone heard was the famous "Shot Heard 'Round the World." Thomson hit a three-run homer, and the Giants won the pennant.

CORNER OF FAME

Mickey Mantle.

The Mick was the greatest switch-hitting slugger in baseball history. In a career plagued with leg injuries and illnesses, he still hit 536 home runs, many of them tape-measure shots. He won the AL Triple Crown in 1956, when he led the league in batting (.353), home runs (52), and RBIs (130). When his legs were young, he was also considered the fastest player in the game. Mantle collected 2,415 hits in his eighteen-year career, all with the Yankees. He was voted MVP three times, and holds the World Series home run record with 18. He was elected to the Hall of Fame in 1974.

> *Do not find fault with the umpires. You cannot expect them to be as perfect as you are.*
> —*Joe McCarthy*

PITCHING TOTALS

PLAYER	G	GS	W	L	PCT	IP	H	R	ER	BB	SO	ERA	SV

WHEN I WAS A KID

Ty Cobb, Outfield, Detroit, Philadelphia (AL), 1905–28. Batted .400 three times, 4,191 career hits. Hall of Fame, 1936.

"My glove was a disgrace. It was just a tattered piece of leather I'd sewn together. Down at the dry-goods store was a model I couldn't live without. But I didn't dare ask my father to buy it.

"Slipping into my father's library, I selected two of his more expensive books, traded them for the glove, and complimented myself on a deal well made. It wasn't stealing, the way I saw it. The library contained books by the score. I had no

glove. The exchange was merited. Anyway, who'd notice the volumes were missing?

"Professor Cobb did. And he took another view of it. . . .

" 'Tyrus,' he said. 'I want to talk to you.' He led me into the library and shut the door.

"Let us draw the curtain of mercy over the scene."

* * *

Stanley Coveleski, Pitcher, Cleveland and others. 1912, 1916–28. Five-time 20-game winner. Hall of Fame, 1969.

"I was born in 1890 in Shamokin, Pennsylvania. When I was 12,

I was working in the [coal] mines from seven in the morning to seven at night, six days a week. . . .

"I never played much baseball in those days. I couldn't. But every evening after I got home, I'd throw stones at tin cans. Just for something to do. I'd put a tin can on a log, or tie it to a tree, and stand maybe forty or fifty feet away and throw stones at it. I did that for so many years, I could hit those things blindfolded.

"Well, the semipro team in town heard about me and asked if I'd like to pitch for them. . . . I was signed to a contract, and I was out of those mines for good."

GLOSSARY OF BASEBALL LINGO

ACE. The best pitcher on a team. Baseball's first pro team, the Cincinnati Red Stockings, had a pitcher named Asa Brainard who was so good that his record in 1869 was 65–0 with one tie. Some say that in his honor, a good pitcher came to be called an Asa. This was later shortened to ace. More likely, though, the term comes from playing cards in which the ace is the best of the bunch. In baseball's earliest days, the 1840s and '50s, men who came around the bases to touch home plate scored an *ace*, not a run. An ace is also called the *stopper*, because he will stop a team's losing streak.

AROUND THE HORN. When the ball is thrown around the infield after an out with no one on base, it's called throwing it "around the horn." The saying comes from the trip ships used to have to take all the way around Cape Horn at the tip of South America before the Panama Canal was built.

BALTIMORE CHOP. A batted ball that hits in front of home plate and bounces high into the air. In the 1890s, the Baltimore Orioles kept their park's infield very hard and made many hits this way.

BATTERY. A pitcher and catcher pairing. It comes from the military term for a group of big guns that are fired together.

BUSH LEAGUE. In old minor league ballparks the fields were usually in poor condition, with weeds and sometimes shrubs growing out of the grass. Today, any crude or immature behavior in baseball is called "bush league" or "bush."

CAN OF CORN. An easy pop fly. In old-style grocery stores, cans were piled high on shelves. When the grocer needed a can of corn, he would tip the top one with a stick and it would fall easily into his hands.

CLEANUP. The fourth-place hitter in the lineup. He is usually the team's most powerful hitter and is expected to "clean up" the bases by driving baserunners home.

CLUTCH. A big hit or a big play in the field made when the outcome of the game depends upon it.

COLLAR. A batter who fails to get a hit in a game wears the collar. It refers to the heavy collars that wagon horses had to wear.

CLOTHES LINE. A hard-hit line drive. Also called a *frozen rope*.

DINGER. A home run. Also, a *tater*, short for *long tater*, which comes from *long potatoes*, an expression that began in the Negro Leagues.

FIREMAN. A team's best relief pitcher, he usually comes into a game with men on base and a big hitter at bat. He's there to put out the fire.

FUNGO. The practice game when a player throws the ball into the air and bats it himself. Long ago, the batter would yell, "One go, two goes, fun goes."

GOPHER BALL. The Yankees' Lefty Gomez said it was any bad pitch that would "go for a home run."

GUN. A great arm, usually belonging to an outfielder, infielder, or catcher.

HUMMER. A good fastball that seems to make a humming sound as it goes by. Infielders will sometimes encourage a fastball pitcher by saying "Hum, babe." Also *heater, heat, gas,* and *mustard,* as in "He really had some mustard on that pitch."

HIT FOR THE CYCLE. When a batter gets a single, double, triple, and home run in one game.

HOT CORNER. The third baseman is said to play "the hot corner" because he has to field a lot of hard-hit line drives and grounders, even though he plays so close to the batter.

HOT DOG. A player who likes to show off. Also *hot shot.*

KEYSTONE. Second base. In architecture, the keystone is the important center stone at the top of an arch. Second base is the center of the infield defense. The second baseman and shortstop are called the "keystone combination."

ON DECK. The batter waiting to hit next is on deck. In the navy, to be "on deck" means to be ready.

PEPPER. A practice game where a player tosses a ball to a player with a bat who taps it to another player and so on. It's called "pepper" because it's lively.

SHOESTRING CATCH. A catch by an outfielder where he must run in and grab the ball "right off his shoe tops." It could also be called a *circus catch*, which refers to any acrobatic grab.

SOUTHPAW. A lefthanded thrower. Ballparks were once built with home plate at the west end so that batters would not have the afternoon sun in their eyes. Pitchers faced west, so their left arms were on the south side.

STEPPING IN THE BUCKET. This comes from the days when teams used to keep a water bucket on the top step of the dugout. When a batter steps away from the plate with his front foot while he swings—an indication that he is frightened by the inside pitch and looking toward the security of the bench—he is "stepping into the bucket."

TEXAS LEAGUER. A softly hit ball that falls just over an infielder's head and just in front of an outfielder for a hit. Art Sunday, a onetime star with Houston in the Texas League, hit .390 for Toledo in the International League in 1890, but many of his hits were those "in-betweeners." A sportswriter began calling them "Texas League hits." Similar to a *wounded duck*, a fly ball that dies just past the infield and falls in for a hit.

TAPE MEASURE SHOT. A long home run, well past the fences.

TOOLS OF IGNORANCE. A catcher's equipment. In the old days, catchers were kidded about being dumb, because why else would anyone want to do such a tough job? Muddy Ruel, a catcher who was a lawyer in the off season, jokingly called his mask, chest protector, and shin guards the tools of ignorance.

WORM-BURNER. A hard-hit ground ball that rolls low and fast over the infield grass.

YAKKER. A curveball. Named for a bird, the yawker, that would suddenly change direction in flight. Curveballs have lots of names. A sharp-breaking curveball is also called a *yellow hammer*, after another unpredictable bird. A big, bending curveball is called a *jughandle* if it comes from over the top, and a *roundhouse* if it comes from the side. And a curveball that is simply outstanding is called *Uncle Charlie*—just out of respect.

AUTOGRAPHS

We hope you'll use these pages to collect the autographs of your favorite players. Here are a few tips on the best way to get them:

- Mind your manners. Say please and thank you. Be patient if the player asks you to wait. Ballplayers are just regular people. If you are nice to them, they'll be nice to you.
- The best time to approach a player is about thirty minutes before the game, after he's warmed up. Another good time is outside the players' entrance to the stadium before or after the game—except if it's a getaway game and he has a bus to catch.
- If you spot a player in a restaurant, don't interrupt his meal. That's just plain rude. Either catch him before he sits down or as he is getting up to leave.
- Don't be greedy. Ask for one autograph. Two, at the most. And have your pen and paper ready.
- Don't send your parents over to get the autograph for you. Players like kids, really. Especially nice kids.

AUTOGRAPHS

AUTOGRAPHS